BIRD
IDENTIFICATION
& FIELDCRAFT

Ivan Nethercoat and Mike Langman
Introduction by Bill Oddie

HAMLYN

For Sarah and Katie.

With thanks to Karen, and to Jo and Sam for making it happen. Both Ivan and Mike would like to thank all the YOC leaders who stirred their interest in birds as YOC members, particularly Tommy Upton, Joyce and Harry Blake and Conway Longworth-Dames.

First published in 1994 by Hamlyn Limited,
an imprint of Reed Consumer Books Limited
Michelin House, 81 Fulham Road, London SW3 6RB
and Auckland, Melbourne, Singapore and Toronto.

Copyright © Reed International Books Limited 1994

Text copyright © Ivan Nethercoat 1994
Illustrations copyright © Mike Langman 1994
Photographs copyright © see page 48.

ISBN 0 600 57963 8

A CIP catalogue record for this book is available from the British Library.

Cover photograph: Goldfinch by Paul Sterry (Nature Photographers Ltd)
Back cover photograph by C H Gomersall (RSPB).
Cover illustrations by Mike Langman.

CONTENTS

BILL ODDIE'S INTRODUCTION

Grown ups love droning on about how different and difficult things were when they were young. Well, when it comes to birdwatching, it's true! I was about seven when I managed to persuade my Dad to buy me my first pair of binoculars. That was over 40 years ago and there were no bird magazines or specialist optical shops. I was lucky I didn't end up with a plastic toy pair! In fact, my first binoculars were very good and lasted for years, so Dad must have taken good advice from somewhere.

But how did I know how and where to go birdwatching? And how did I know what I was looking at? The only real identification book available then was the *Observer's Book of Birds* which didn't even have all the British birds in it, let alone pictures of them in all their different plumages. It was not until 1954, when I was thirteen that the first 'modern' fieldguide came out.

And yet, I like to think that, by the time I became a teenager, I wasn't a bad birdwatcher. So, how did I do it? Well, by experience. Nearly every day, I used to walk to the woods and around the golf course (watching out for flying balls as well as birds). Every weekend, I would cycle to the local reservoir or persuade my Dad to give me a lift. And I'd campaign to take our family holidays in Norfolk or Devon so I could see some new species. I spent an amazing amount of time, but looking back, I probably wasted a lot, too, making mistakes that I could have avoided if only there had been books like this one.

This book deals with bird identification and fieldcraft. It will help you avoid the mistakes I made and make the best of the time you spend birdwatching. After all, you may not be able to get out as much as I did. There are so many other things to do these days aren't there? Personal stereos, video games, computers ... we didn't have any of those when I was a lad. Oops, sorry. There I go again!

Yes, things have changed, but whatever your age, there are three undeniable facts. Firstly, there are birds everywhere (even in the middle of a city). Secondly, there is no substitute for getting out there and seeing birds for yourself. And, thirdly, birdwatching is a hobby for life. I'm still at it. Never give it up.

Bill Oddie

INTRODUCTION

Tony Soper once said 'Life is never boring for a birdwatcher' and I agree. I have been interested in birds and other wildlife since the age of about seven and, after 25 years, I still enjoy going out to watch birds.

There are few hobbies that you will be able to do almost anywhere but birdwatching is one of them. You can watch birds from your bedroom window, from a bus, a boat, a train, while on holiday, in your school playground ...

This book tells you what to look for, how to get close enough to see birds properly and how to find them in the first place! It is for anyone who wants to learn the basics of how to identify birds and get the most out of their birdwatching.

The number of different types of birds you will recognize will grow as you find out more about them. Watch birds whenever you get the chance and get to know how they move and behave.

A great way to learn more is to watch a 'local patch' and keep a notebook. Find an area near your home where you can go birdwatching – try a local park or wood – and go as often as you can. Make rough sketches and notes about the birds you see each time you visit. You will soon learn to tell the difference between a House Sparrow and a Hedge Sparrow and, once you can identify the common species, you will notice if anything unusual turns up.

You do not need a powerful telescope, a flashy pair of binoculars or special clothes to watch birds. Anyone can birdwatch, but how well you do it depends on how good your identification and fieldcraft skills are. Read on and take a step towards a less boring life ...

FIELDCRAFT

Birds have extremely good eyesight and hearing and, at the slightest hint of danger, they will disappear from view. Good fieldcraft helps you to find birds and see them well without disturbing them. Much is common sense and will become second nature with practice.

The best way to see birds well is to get to know your subject and practise. Reading about birds in a fieldguide or other type of bird book is an important way to learn more but nothing beats experience 'in the field'.

First of all, find out if there is a junior section of your local natural history society or bird club or, better still, a local group of the Young Ornithologists' Club (YOC), the junior section of the Royal Society for the Protection of Birds. You will then be able to go out with experienced birdwatchers.

It sometimes seems as though birdwatchers have super eyesight that gives them the ability to see birds in apparently empty

bushes and identify tiny black dots in the sky. In reality, their eyesight is unlikely to be any better than yours but years of practice have given them the ability to pick up the slightest signs of movement that may give away a bird's presence. They will also know what birds are likely to be seen in different habitats. Practice will give you the ability to concentrate on sights and sounds around you – vital clues to a bird's whereabouts.

Start early whenever possible. Birds are generally most active early in the morning. Keep looking for signs of movement and talk and move quietly. If you see a bird that you don't recognize and need to get closer, you need to be able to 'stalk' the bird like a hunter or American Indian scout. Pick your

Your garden or local park can be a great place to birdwatch. Notice how the different species move and behave and learn to spot movements in hedges and bushes as birds approach a birdtable.

A Chaffinch at a pond (above).

You will see more birds where there is a mixture of habitats. Keep still and quiet and the birds will soon ignore you.

route carefully and use whatever cover you can, even if it means crouching or crawling. Choose your route so that, when you finish, you are not looking into the sun and do not try to get too close – the welfare of birds must always come first

Learn to walk quietly and slowly, keeping your eyes and ears open to any sounds or movement. If you see something move in trees or bushes, stop and have a closer look. It may not be a bird, just a leaf blowing in the wind or a branch moving, but the important thing is that you are aware of movement. Similarly, if you hear a bird song or call that you do not recognize, go and find out what it is, don't ignore it!

As well as the ability to concentrate, you will need a certain amount of patience. Often, the best way to see birds is to let them come to you. Birds are very sensitive to movement but will often ignore a stationary object. If you stop, keep still and watch a bush or tree where you see movement, the chances are that the bird will soon ignore you and show itself. Whatever you do, do not throw things to try and 'flush' a bird out.

If you have time, combine a 'wait and see' approach with a slow walk, especially in areas of dense cover like a wood or reedbed.

But choose your viewpoint with care. Birds are often easiest to see where two or more types of habitat meet, such as woodland clearings or edges of pools. Here there will be a greater variety of food and, therefore, more birds and, at the edge of the reedbed or woodland, they will be easier to see.

So, if your route takes you into a woodland clearing, sit down and wait to see what comes into view. If you go out in a car, don't forget that it can make an excellent and comfortable 'hide'. Birds will soon ignore it and often come remarkably close.

One of the best places to practise watching birds is in your garden or local park. The birds will be used to people and you will be able to watch them closely.

Feed birds in winter and plant shrubs and flowers that are good for wildlife in your garden and you will encourage birds to visit. See how they fly or walk and get used to their general behaviour and appearance. This will give you a valuable source of information that will help you identify more unusual birds later.

Once you really start to watch all the birds in your garden or park, you will be surprised at the number of different species that you recognize. You will see that not all birds are

Hat to keep
head warm

Gloves

Scarf

Light
windproof
jacket

Drawstring
to trap heat

Large
pockets for
notebook

Wear thick
socks with
wellies

It is important to be warm and comfortable in winter.

If you sit in a hide on a nature reserve, you will be able to watch birds in comfort. Remember, though, to keep quiet – not many hides are sound-proofed!

the same and you will find that you notice small differences.

Clothing

Birdwatching should be fun. It is difficult to enjoy yourself if you are too hot or too cold so make sure you are wearing the right clothes. In winter it can get very cold, especially on estuaries or reservoirs, so warm, waterproof clothing is essential. Colour isn't too important but avoid bright or fluorescent colours and dress in several layers rather than one thick coat.

Wear a scarf and a light windproof and waterproof jacket over two or three layers and you will be comfortable and able to take layers off if the weather changes. Wrap a scarf around your neck and use a drawstring waist to trap air against your body to keep you warm. A hat is also useful to keep your head warm and better than a hood because you'll still be able to hear the birds.

Waterproof boots can be useful but good ones are expensive. Wellies are all right if you are not planning to walk too far but they can be very cold and your feet may sweat. Light, fabric walking boots with a good sole are warmer but are not totally waterproof unless they are lined with GoreTex. But these are expensive and the waterproofing does not last for ever. (GoreTex doesn't work properly when it has been stretched by your foot.)

In hot weather, you should wear clothes that will protect your skin and keep you cool. Again, wear whatever you feel comfortable in. If it is very hot, you'll need to drink water to stop you dehydrating. A hat will protect your eyes, keep you cool and help to stop you from getting headaches.

Whatever you wear, remember that you will need a pocket to carry your notebook. A small, lightweight rucksack is also useful for carrying a drink, food and clothes.

Hides

Most nature reserves have a well-positioned hide so you can get good, close-up views of birds in relative comfort without having to spend time 'stalking'. This does not mean that you will not need to practise any field-craft to see birds well. Birds can still be easily frightened from a hide. So remember:

■ Be as quiet as possible when approaching and leaving hides.

■ Do not point out of the windows: birds will eventually ignore things that don't move so make sure they don't see your arms waving or your binoculars moving.

■ Give accurate directions to people so they can locate birds. Use the 'clock method'.

■ Unless the hide has a screened door, try not to open doors and windows together. The birds will be able to see into the hide and may fly further away.

■ Remember to look out for birds on the paths between the hides.

Try to get hold of information about the reserve before you visit so you can plan your route to make the most of the light and the time of day. This is particularly important on

Twitching can be exciting but do not forget to watch birds in your local patch. Make sure you really get to know the common species.

a coastal reserve where you will also need to know the tide times. Of course, not every site that you visit will have hides but a nature reserve leaflet should tell you the types of birds you are likely to see. Use this to work out what to expect and look for and you will have a much more rewarding time.

Twitching

For some people, seeing rare birds has become a separate hobby and, occasionally, an obsession. By telephoning special (and expensive!) numbers birdwatchers can get details of and directions to the latest sightings. While it can be great fun going on the occasional 'twitch', it can be very frustrating, especially if the bird is hard to see or has flown off just before you arrive!

There is little point in building up a great list of rare birds that you have seen if you are unfamiliar with common species. Before you persuade someone to take you to see an Olive-backed Pipit, for example, make sure you are familiar with Tree and Meadow Pipits. If you do go on a 'twitch', use your skills so you are confident that the bird you see is what everyone says it is.

The 'clock method' : Here, 12 o'clock is straight ahead, the Cormorant is at 1 o'clock and the Avocet is at 10 o'clock. Or, looking from the hide on the far bank, the Avocet is at 5 o'clock !

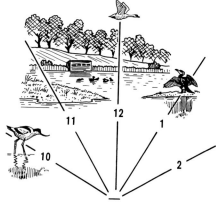

EQUIPMENT

Binoculars come in two main designs: porroprism (above) and roof prism (below). Roof prism binoculars are more compact but good ones are more expensive than porroprism binoculars.

You do not need masses of expensive equipment to watch birds. To start off, all you need is a notebook, a pencil and your eyesight. However, if you are going to take your birdwatching seriously, sooner or later you will need a pair of binoculars.

Whatever the design, binoculars are described in the same way: usually 8 × 30, 10 × 50, or something similar. These numbers are the 'specification': the first one tells you the magnification and the second tells you the diameter of the objective lens (the large lens, farthest from the eyepiece). With a pair of 8 × binoculars, what you see will be 8 times larger than what you see with the naked eye.

In theory, the larger the second number, the better because it will let in more light. In practice, though, this may not be the case because the quality of the image also depends on the quality of the lenses.

Generally, the more expensive the binoculars, the better they are. A cheap pair of 8 × 40 binoculars probably will not be as good as an expensive pair of 8 × 20. This is important to remember, don't just buy binoculars on the strength of the specification alone.

The golden rule for anyone buying binoculars, even the most expensive type, is 'try before you buy'. If the shop will not let you take them outside to test, take your custom elsewhere. There are several specialist binocular shops that will be happy for you to try out and compare different types. They will also advise you on the best pair for you. Birdwatching magazines will have details of dealers and special open days.

Second-hand binoculars can be excellent value for money if the optics inside are all right. Do not worry about the odd

Telescopes are not essential and always need extra support, such as a tripod. They are useful when looking at birds in the distance or to see birds really closely.

Drawtube telescope   Prismatic telescope

A good pair of binoculars will help you to see birds like this Redshank clearly without getting too close.

scratch on the outside. Ask your dealer if there are any you can try.

When you are testing binoculars outside, you will need to adjust them for your own eyes (see How to Use Binoculars below). The image you see should be one clear, sharp circle. Look at objects like television aerials or fine branches against a bright sky – this will show up any defects such as colour fringing or double vision.

Birdwatching binoculars should be very comfortable to use and easy on your eyes (if you get headaches, there is something wrong). They should not be too heavy and no more than 10 ×. You may find that you see more clearly through a pair of 7 × or 8 × because they will be easier to hold steady. Also, the lower the magnification, the wider the field of view. Avoid zoom binoculars for birdwatching.

Once you have a pair of binoculars, you need to practise so that using them becomes second nature. When you see a bird, you need to be able to bring your binoculars to your eyes without taking your eyes off the bird and find it straight away. Practise using them in the garden or indoors. Focus on nearby and distant objects and learn how to hold them steady.

Always take great care when cleaning your binoculars. Never use your fingers to wipe the lenses because they can damage the glass coating. Use a soft cotton cloth or special tissue and first blow off any grit which could scratch the lenses. Take care near the coast: sand and salt spray can be damaging.

Telescopes

If you decide to buy a telescope, again make sure you get it from a specialist shop. Many models are just not suitable.

Whatever telescope you buy, you will need a tripod to keep it steady. Telescopes are too heavy to hold by hand. All this equipment will be expensive and a lot to carry around so do buy with care. It is much better to get a really good pair of binoculars than cheap binoculars, a telescope and tripod.

HOW TO USE BINOCULARS

1 Pick a well-defined object, like a car number plate.
2 Close your right eye and focus the binoculars using the central wheel.
3 Close your left eye and focus your right eye by turning the adjustable eye piece.
4 Make a note of its position.
5 Now focus for both eyes using the central wheel as necessary.

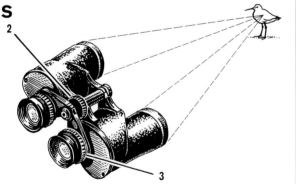

IDENTIFICATION

Familiarizing yourself with the common or regular species of birds is an important first step in identification. Get to know the way they behave 'in the field' as well as the way they appear in the fieldguides. Once you know the common species well, any new or unusual birds will really stand out.

First, make sure that you have a good fieldguide and get to know your way around it really well. In nearly all fieldguides, the different families of birds appear in the same order, starting with divers and grebes and ending up with the buntings. A good fieldguide will tell you where and when to expect to see birds and will be an invaluable source of information.

There are many different fieldguides, some are awful, most are very good but none of them are perfect! Those published by Hamlyn, Collins, Macmillan and Helm, for example, are all good but each has some bad points. It is a good idea to have more than one fieldguide: you get a range of information and illustrations from different experts.

As a general rule, your fieldguide should have good quality pictures that show at least all the British birds in a variety of plumages, both sexes and different ages. Photographic guides seldom make good fieldguides.

As well as fieldguides, there are many other excellent reference books on all aspects of birds and their behaviour, and many wildlife films on video and even video guides to identification (avoid those that show only drawings). Many of these are expensive so you could take a trip to your library to see what's on offer.

The second and most important way to get to know the birds around you is the simplest and cheapest. Spend time watching the birds that come near your home.

People often say that they get nothing but sparrows and Starlings in their garden but if they took the time to watch they would probably see many more species. Put up a bird-table and provide food and water regularly and you will be surprised at the number of different species that visit.

When you start to study birds closely, you will notice that many of them move, fly and feed in very different ways. Each has its own characteristics and behaviour which will give you an overall impression of the bird and give clues to its identity.

Jizz

Often all you will see is a fleeting glimpse or a silhouette and you'll have no time to look for colours or fieldmarks. With experience, you can often make a good guess at what it is by knowing what birds to expect and its overall size, shape, behaviour and posture. These give each species its own 'jizz'.

If you look at the photograph below, you will start to get a feel for what jizz is. Even though it is white, you can still tell it is a Blackbird – the way the bird is standing and its overall characteristics show this. Plumage and colour can not hide the bird's identity. You can also see this in the silhouettes on pages 16 and 17, where, although they are black, you can still identify them.

By noting the jizz, obvious fieldmarks and voice of a bird, you will be able to identify nearly all the birds you see.

Familiarizing yourself with common birds is very important, so do not stop looking at Kestrels or Willow Warblers just because you have seen them before. It is knowing the common birds well that will help you identify birds quickly.

This albino Blackbird (above) still looks like a Blackbird because its general size, shape and characteristics, or 'jizz', is just right.

Studying birds in your garden or park will help you to get to know the habits and behaviour of several species. Watch how they fly, walk, run and feed – each bird is different.

Getting to know common birds, such as Kestrels (below right), will mean that you will identify more unusual species, like Peregrines.

Waders and birds of prey are groups of birds that can be tricky to identify unless you recognize the common species.

Kestrels are found in the same habitats where you could see a Merlin, Hobby or Peregrine. To be sure of identifying any of them, get to know all the features of Kestrels. You can see them almost anywhere. They regularly hunt their prey of voles or mice by hovering for long periods over rough grassland. Next time you travel along a motorway, look for them hunting over grass verges or the central reservation. Watch them flying between bouts of hovering and get used to their distinctive silhouette.

The Peregrine is another well-known bird of prey. It is much rarer and not as widespread as the Kestrel. It often soars very high up, waiting for some unsuspecting prey to fly below. Being a much more powerful bird, It feeds on much larger prey and will take birds the size of a pigeon by doing its world-famous 100 mph 'stoop'.

You will often see birds of prey as black shapes high in the sky or flying very fast and low. Identification is often a process of elimination based on behaviour and silhouette and these are often more important to spot than plumage details: you will find it almost impossible to judge the colours accurately. Get to know Kestrels, Sparrowhawks and, if you can, Buzzards, and you should be able to have a go at identifying birds of prey anywhere in Europe.

Picking out a juvenile Curlew Sandpiper (centre) from a flock of waders can be tricky unless you get to know Dunlins well.

Waders are another group of birds that can cause real identification problems. It is easy to confuse the plumages of juveniles and many similarly sized and coloured birds when they are all together. For most of the regular species that breed in Britain or feed and rest on estuaries in winter, it is not too difficult to identify them if you get to know their habits and what to expect to see when. Avocets and Oystercatchers are normally easy to identify but the smaller, less obvious birds can be a problem.

One of the commonest waders in Britain is the Dunlin. Many thousands of adults and young birds visit our shores in the autumn and will be in a range of plumages. At an estuary nature reserve, you may see them feeding quite close to hides but normally you will see them as tiny dots running over the mud or taking to the air in huge flocks. It is important to know Dunlins' jizz and different plumages. This will help you pick out waders like Sanderlings and Curlew Sandpipers.

Do not feel that you have to be right every time, getting experience means making mistakes and asking questions. Everyone makes mistakes, even with common species. There are many stories about famous identification mistakes made by experts. Plastic bags have been confidently identified as harriers or owls and, once, a bus was pointed out as an eagle to a crowd of twitchers!

Size

While it seems a simple thing to describe, it can be very difficult to estimate size in the field. It is even more difficult to judge when you realize that your binoculars magnify everything you see.

All the measurements in bird books are taken as though the bird were dead and lying flat on its back on a ruler. This is not a situation that you will come across very often! Even two birds the same length may look very different in the field because of the way they stand and move.

Unless you can compare a bird directly with another one nearby it is difficult to be accurate. It is much better to describe it as 'roughly Sparrow-sized', 'Blackbird-sized' or 'pigeon-sized' than to worry too much about centimetres.

Two other sizes that you will often see in fieldguides, especially in the section on birds of prey, are wingspan and wing length. Wingspan is the distance between the two wingtips when the bird has its wings stretched out. Wing length is not half this distance, it is the length from the wing tip to the carpal joint, the equivalent of our elbow.

Beak shape

One of the reasons that birds are so successful is that they have evolved to feed in many different ways. If all the birds that visited your garden ate the same food, in the same way, there would not be enough to go round. The severe competition would mean that only the strongest would survive. To avoid this, different species have evolved different ways of feeding.

The beaks of birds are one of their most important identification features. The picture on the right shows some of the different beak shapes and sizes, from the small, insect-eating Blue Tit to the powerful, flesh-tearing beak of the Buzzard.

Even within a group of birds, the variety can be enormous. Our estuaries are home to thousands of waders each year and the reason that they can all feed together is that they feed in different ways on different food. Have a look at the beak shapes of the Curlew and the Redshank. The Curlew can reach deep into the sand or mud and feed on animals that are out of reach for the Redshank.

Look in your fieldguide at the wide variety of beak shapes and see how they vary among groups of birds, like waders and warblers.

Fieldguides

If you see a bird that you do not recognize, do not rush for your fieldguide first. It is much better to make quick notes of its shape, colour, behaviour, approximate size, etc. in a notebook. Make a rough sketch of it, too. Once you have collected as much information as you can, then look in your fieldguide to find out what it could be. Make sure you

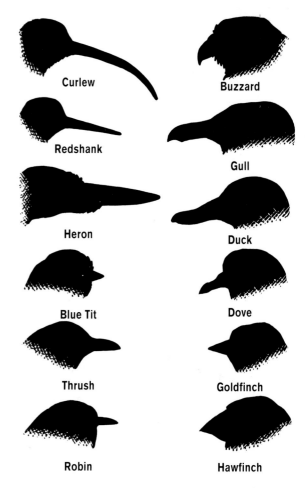

Birds' beaks are one of their most important features. The variety is enormous and they are an important clue to the family the bird belongs to

read the descriptions of the birds as well as looking at the pictures.

Different bird artists have their own style and, despite the fact that most fieldguides have most of the same birds in them, they each have their own feel. Ask other birdwatchers' advice on which fieldguide is best and buy one that covers the area you want.

If you are new to birdwatching, you do not really need a fieldguide that covers every bird seen in Europe. It would be much better to buy one that includes the different plumages of birds in north-west Europe, such as ducks in their eclipse plumage.

There are lots of good fieldguides (right). Choose one that covers all the British species with several pictures showing a range of plumages. The descriptions should tell you where and when to expect to see the birds and something about the way they behave.

You can recognize many birds by their shape and characteristics, not just their plumage.

Pied Wagtail

Robin

Starling

Blackbird

Wren

Blue Tit

Great Tit

Chaffinch

A good fieldguide will have descriptions and maps to show where birds live opposite the pictures. Choose a fieldguide that has paintings of birds rather than photographs. Paintings show a lot more detail.

If you are just starting to birdwatch and you live in Britain, the best fieldguides to buy are those that cover Britain and Ireland only. *The Shell Guide to the Birds of Britain and Ireland* and the *RSPB Guide to British Birds* are two of my favourites but there are others. You can get one that covers the rest of Europe when you are a bit more experienced.

It is not just the pictures that are important. Make sure that the fieldguide you want includes good descriptions of the birds, details of where and when you can expect to see them and maps to show where they spend the summer and winter.

FIELDMARKS

Once you start to notice birds, you will soon realize that there is a remarkable range of sizes, shapes, colours and patterns, even among the commonest birds. In many species, groups of feathers form distinct patterns that can help you identify them.

All birds have their feathers arranged in the same way. Whether they are Goldcrests or Golden Eagles, their feather tracts will be the same although the number of feathers in each will vary.

Knowing the correct name and they way these feathers lie can be very important in identifying some species and when writing notes on plumage. A good fieldguide will show you the main fieldmarks you need to note, but it is also useful to look at close-up photographs of birds.

Look at the diagrams on these pages and see how they relate to the feather patterns on the birds in the photographs. Get to know how feathers look and you will be able to spot them when you are birdwatching.

Some birds have very distinctive fieldmarks that give instant clues to their identity. The Wheatear (left) and the Bullfinch (right) show white rumps as they fly off.

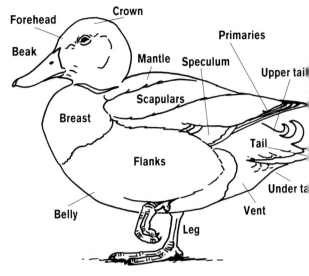

Birds have the same groups of feathers, but in ducks and waders, some are more obvious.

This, of course, assumes that you see a bird well enough to see a lot of detail. It is more likely that you will get one of those fleeting glimpses, but even then you will often notice some fieldmarks.

The white rumps of Bullfinches and Wheatears are easy to see when they fly and, in a flock of finches in winter, this may be what you need to first spot a lone Brambling.

Wingbars and tail feathers can be very distinctive, as on Chaffinches and Redstarts. The shape of the tail may also be an important field characteristic, as in the forked tails of birds such as kites, Swallows, terns and some finches.

The shape of the beak will give clues to the type of food a bird eats and the family it belongs to: the small, fine bills of birds like warblers are designed for picking up insects; the stubby, fat beaks of finches and sparrows for seeds; and the sharp, hooked beaks of birds of prey for tearing up flesh. A bird is designed to fit into its place in the food chain and its shape, characteristics and features will give you clues.

Practise naming the feather tracts on birds from good photographs (like the female House Sparrow, left). Learning the various names helps when identifying birds and is important if you want to make an accurate record of what you see.

Compare the drawing below with the 'fieldguide' illustration (below right) to see how the feather tracts produce the distinctive patterns seen as fieldmarks.

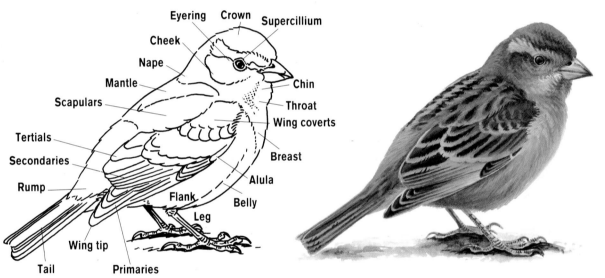

Eyering   Crown   Supercillium
Cheek
Nape
Mantle
Scapulars
Tertials
Secondaries
Rump
Wing tip
Tail   Primaries
Leg
Flank   Belly
Alula
Breast
Wing coverts
Throat
Chin

Some of the most distinctive head markings are those around the eye. Eyestripes can go through or above the eye or both, as in the Firecrest; or, if you get a really close view, you may see that the eye itself is coloured or has a coloured ring. Some birds have distinctive moustachial stripes as in a few of the buntings.

The wings will often have fieldmarks that are very distinctive. Wingbars are formed by the white feather tips of the coverts and can be very obvious, as in Chaffinches. In some species of ducks, you will see well-marked wings, especially when the bird is in flight.

Tufted Ducks have very obvious wingbars and Goldeneyes and Wigeons have large wing patches. Some ducks also have a large patch of white or brightly coloured feathers in the secondaries. This is the speculum and can be an important fieldmark to look out for.

The shape of the wings will also vary with the bird's lifestyle. The Barn Owl, for example, has long wings for gliding and flying over open fields while the Tawny Owl has shorter, fatter wings so it can fly among trees. Even on the smallest birds, the wing shape can be surprisingly obvious if you know to look out for it.

LIGHT EFFECTS

When you start to look at birds in the field, remember that books are only a guide and that light can make a bird look very different.

Bright sunlight can be a problem if you want to examine a bird's colour and markings. It produces a very contrasty light that can hide important fieldmarks or make colours look completely different. Glossy black feathers can look white, for example, and strong shadows can turn browns into black.

Lightly overcast light is often better because you will be able to pick out the colour differences more easily. If it is sunny, try to keep the sun behind you and, if you can, pick your route to make sure that you

A real Kestrel may look quite different from the picture in your fieldguide (above). Birds can look very different depending on the light you see them in. A Kestrel perched in bright light (left) will look quite different when flying against a bright sky (below). With few colours visible, the silhouette and behaviour are important clues to identification.

do not see the birds as silhouettes. If you cannot change the direction of your walk, change the time of day that you visit. If a site faces east, it will be unsuitable for watching from in the morning, but in the evening the sun will be behind you.

The effect of light on a bird's surroundings will also affect what you see. Light reflecting off a pale-coloured surface will illuminate the underside of a bird and a pale bird flying against a brightly lit sea or sky may appear quite dark.

There are no hard and fast rules, just be aware that a bird can look very different depending on the lighting conditions. Always take the light into account when you are making notes. It could be that, because of the light, you will not be able to make out some plumage detail that appeared to be obvious in your fieldguide. Waders seen across an estuary on a dull afternoon will look very different on a bright morning.

If you go birdwatching abroad, remember, too, that the light may be quite different from what you are used to in this country. Even familiar birds can look very different. First-time visitors to the Mediterranean often identify Kestrels as Lesser Kestrels because the bright light sometimes makes the birds look very pale underneath.

The Redpoll appears to be well-marked and colourful in a fieldguide (above left) but may look quite different when you see one in the top of a bush against the light (above). See how different the two Redpolls in these photographs look.

PLUMAGE AND MOULT

A bird's feathers are vital to its survival. They allow it to fly, keep it warm and can protect it from danger by camouflage. All birds take a great deal of care of their feathers by bathing and preening regularly but eventually feathers do wear out and need to be replaced. This is a process called moult.

Different species moult in different ways and during the process the bird can look very different from the 'perfect' pictures you see in a fieldguide.

No book shows all the different plumages a bird can go through. Most of them only show those the bird has in summer or in winter. Even then, it is sometimes only the male that is shown because he is usually the more brightly coloured.

All birds go through at least two different plumages. They have one when they are newly hatched and have their first full set of feathers (this juvenile plumage is usually well-camouflaged so it does not attract predators), and a different set when they are fully grown adults. In some birds, such as gulls, the number of different plumages may be much greater, and in some of the eagles it can take many years before a bird gets its full set of adult feathers.

The way the feathers are moulted varies between different species. Generally, the moult is either partial, where only some of the feathers are lost, or complete where all the feathers are replaced over several weeks.

Just before and during moulting a bird can look very tatty with many feathers either badly worn or missing, or it can take on a mixture of adult and juvenile plumages. Some waders, for example, start moulting in their breeding grounds in the Arctic, stop for a while as they migrate to their winter feeding areas and then continue. When we first see them, they can look very strange and not at all like they do in a fieldguide.

1 Juvenile
Black-headed gull

3 First summer

5 Adult in summer

2 First winter

4 Adult in winter

6 Adult moulting

Most birds lose the important groups of feathers such as flight feathers and tail feathers gradually so that they can still fly to find food and escape danger. During the moulting period, it is not unusual to see birds, such as gulls or birds of prey, with feathers missing which may alter the look of their silhouette.

Ducks, however, are different. After breeding they have a full moult in the summer and lose their flight feathers for a short time. This obviously makes them very vulnerable to predators and so they often flock together until their feathers are replaced.

During this period, the normally brightly coloured males take on a much duller plumage – often similar to the camouflaged colours of the female. This is an 'eclipse' plumage and helps to camouflage the males during their enforced grounding. It is during this period, when males, females and young are all rather drab, that jizz is so important for identification.

As plumage can vary so much from bird to bird, it is unlikely that the birds you see will be exactly like the pictures in a fieldguide, so do treat your fieldguide as just that – a guide. Always take into account the time of year and where you are. Could the bird have just migrated, just hatched or just finished breeding? It might be a young bird or part-way through a moult. Whatever stage of plumage the bird is in, it has the basic shape, size and characteristics of the species.

The Black-headed Gull goes through several stages before it reaches adult plumage. Fieldguides rarely have the space to show them all. Juvenile is the first full plumage the bird develops after hatching. It moults to a first winter plumage after a couple of months. Another moult in spring produces the first summer plumage, with some juvenile feathers in the wings. These are not lost until the bird has another moult taking it into second winter and then to second summer which is the adult plumage. Some non-breeding birds will start to moult before the rest and may start to develop a winter plumage in the summer.

Willow Warblers arrive in this country in a different coloured plumage from the one they leave in! Juveniles (left) are very yellow and, by late summer, both young and adult birds have moulted again (middle and right) before migrating south.

As well as moult changing the colour of a bird from what it looks like in a fieldguide, general wear and tear and the sun will also cause feathers to fade. Towards the end of the breeding season a bird may look much paler than it did in spring.

Some birds use the effects of wear and tear to develop their full breeding plumage. Some of the buntings and finches, for example, moult in the autumn into a plumage where the feathers have wide fringes that are gradually worn away over the winter to reveal more brightly coloured spring plumage underneath.

As plumage can vary so much from bird to bird it is important not to rely too heavily on the colour of a bird when trying to identify it. Always take into account the time of year and make a careful note of its jizz.

If you get the chance, go along to a bird observatory and watch the wardens as they ring birds that have been caught in special traps. You will see that, as well as attaching a ring, the warden carefully measures the bird's beak and wings, and weighs it before it is released.

These measurements help ornithologists to age the birds they catch and to make a positive identification of what could be a rare visitor. For most of us, judging a bird's age is not always easy. Some experienced birdwatchers, however, now know a lot about the different plumages birds go through and, with the aid of telescopes, can tell a bird's age.

A basic knowledge of the process of plumage change is useful and it can really help to tell the difference between some similar-looking species. In spring, telling apart Chiffchaffs and Willow Warblers is extremely difficult unless you hear them singing. They are very similar and any differences in plumage and structure are often hard to see as the birds flit about among leaves. The two birds take on quite different plumages in the autumn, however. In July, Willow Warblers moult into a very yellow plumage. Chiffchaffs moult into a more drab and olive plumage.

Some species have distinct colour varieties. Arctic Skuas can be dark or pale bodied. These variations are often the result of two different populations – or races – of the same species. The Yellow Wagtail that breeds in Britain, is one of many geographical variations of that species. Where two or more races meet, there will be some birds that have bits of both races. The Pied Wagtail is a British race of the continental White Wagtail which often turns up in Britain on migration. It can all get very confusing! A good fieldguide should help you out.

The male Mallard above is in full breeding plumage. Once the breeding season is over, the fine feathers will be worn and tatty and will need to be replaced. He will then moult.

The Brambling's winter feathers have long fringes which are worn down by wear and tear during the winter. After breeding, the bird will moult into its winter plumage again.

During their moult, male ducks take on an 'eclipse' plumage in late summer. This camouflages them from predators while their flight feathers grow back (the two male Mallards above look like females).

The Brambling's breeding plumage (below) is not a result of moulting. Over the winter, the fringes of its winter plumage are worn away to reveal its smart summer feathers.

In some species, such as Buzzards, the plumages of individual birds can vary and they will appear very different. You may see Buzzards that are pale underneath and some that are all dark brown.

Sometimes, though, it may be that a bird has a defect in its plumage. 'Leucism' is a condition that appears when a bird has too few pigments in its feathers and can make a bird look very pale. 'Melanism' is the opposite when a bird can look very dark, or even black.

Albino birds have no colour pigments at all and are all white. While pure albino birds are quite rare, partial albinos, those with a few white feathers, are quite common. Partial albino Blackbirds, for example, are fairly common.

BEHAVIOUR

A bird's behaviour can change its whole appearance and will change at different times of the year, the weather and feeding conditions. Above a Great Crested Grebe is alert (top), getting ready to dive (second), resting (third), and displaying (bottom).

Birds are wonderful animals, full of life and movement, and they can fly! Their behaviour is probably their most obvious feature and more often than not, it is the movement and behaviour of a bird that will attract you to it in the first place. It is this behaviour that can also give you clues to its identity.

Different species of birds move and feed in different ways and you do not always need to see a bird close up to pick out important identification features.

The most obvious aspects of behaviour, apart from singing, are how a bird moves and feeds. Often, the first you will see will be the bird flying away, when you may see distinctive fieldmarks but it is also important to note how the bird flies. Is it in a straight line, like a sparrow, or a deep, bounding flight, like a woodpecker? Once it has stopped, look at how it moves. Does it flick or wag its tail, does it walk or hop? If it is a water bird, how does it swim? Does it dive for fish or weeds? If so, how? All these actions are important to note and you will be able to see them from a distance. You can see the feeding actions of waders, for example, from a long way off and a bird that is feeding differently from the rest will always be worth further investigation.

Birds have two different types of feathers: down and contour. Contour feathers are those that give the bird its shape, such as the flight and tail feathers and those on the coverts and body. The down feathers make up an insulating layer beneath these.

Feathers keep a bird at the right temperature. This is done by the bird puffing its feathers out to keep warm or lying them flat against its body to keep cool. This probably happens automatically depending on the weather, but it can have quite a dramatic effect on the shape of the bird.

Have a look at the birds in your garden or park. In very cold weather, they will look a lot fatter and more squat as they fluff out their down feathers to keep warm. Similarly, if birds are roosting, they will often look fatter than when they are feeding.

Birds of prey are well-known for being difficult to identify. This is not helped by the fact that the main picture in most fieldguides is a colour portrait of the bird perched. Almost every time you see a bird of prey it will be in flight, silhouetted against a bright sky! Identification, therefore, is hardly ever possible from just looking at the plumage. You need to look at differences in shape, structure and behaviour.

Tufted Duck

Shoveler

Mallards

Wigeon

Shoveler

Buzzards and Honey Buzzards are difficult to tell apart because their shapes are very similar. The way a bird flies is a vital clue to which species it is. Honey Buzzards have a flat, soaring flight with occasional 'rowing' wingbeats which is obviously different from the shallow 'v' shape of a soaring Buzzard.

Many small birds also have distinctive behaviour. The wing-flicking of some of the warblers or the tail-wagging of wagtails and others are all important features to look out for. Birds like warblers and pipits can appear to be very similar but their display flights are often quite different. The Meadow Pipit takes to the air from the ground, while the Tree Pipit uses an exposed branch as a perch from which to launch into its familiar 'parachuting' song flight.

Go to a reservoir, old gravel pit or a park lake in the autumn and you will probably see a good selection of ducks, Great Crested

Redshanks (far right) and Spotted Redshanks feed differently and you will be able to see this from a long way off.

Ducks have a wide range of feeding behaviour. Mallards will not dive under the water like Tufted Ducks, but you may be surprised to see a Shoveler diving under water with outstretched wings instead of dabbling at the surface.

Grebes, Coots and Moorhens. Look closely at how they feed and you will see characteristic differences in their behaviour. Mallards will feed near the edge, up-ending to reach plants just below the surface of the water, Shovelers will be sieving through the surface water and Wigeons will probably be grazing the grass

around the edges. Out on the deeper water, Tufted Ducks will be diving under the water for food. Coots, too, will dive down for beakfuls of weed which they bring up to the surface where Gadwalls may be waiting. Gadwalls do not dive and so they wait for Coots to bring weed up, and then take it from them!

Waders, too, adopt many different styles of feeding, even among similar species. Redshanks and Spotted Redshanks are often seen at the same sites in the autumn, but they usually feed in quite different ways. The Spotted Redshanks run about in water up to their bellies while Redshanks feed on the mud, appearing to be afraid to get their feet wet and usually on their own.

You can start to look at the different behaviour patterns of birds from your own garden, especially in winter when many birds will be attracted to a garden that has plenty of food in it. Notice how the different species fly and walk and eat. In spring, watch out for the different displays, ways of building nests and collecting food for young. Most species do each differently.

Strong winds, especially in autumn, can mean that some birds will turn up in unusual places. Visit your local patch to see if there is anything unusual that should not be there. Reservoirs are good places to go after strong gales. Scan the water and look out for anything out of the ordinary. A few years ago, a Leach's Petrel turned up on a large, flooded gravel pit in Bedfordshire after some strong winds had blown it well inland from its usual home in the Atlantic. The pit was also home to several hundred gulls and although the weather was not too good, the bird was easy to spot because of its distinctive feeding behaviour and the fact that it was being mobbed by Black-headed Gulls. If it hadn't been for these two bits of behaviour, a black bird feeding over dark water could have been difficult to pick up.

In autumn and winter, birds are not competing for breeding territories and some species flock for safety from predators and roost together. Many Starlings come to Britain from Scandinavia and huge flocks of thousands of birds roost together in woods or towns. From a distance, the wheeling masses of birds look like wafts of smoke from a fire and it is quite a shock when you realise that the enormous cloud is made up of birds.

Many roosts are smaller and old, thick hedges on farmland are good roosting sites for birds like finches or Long-eared Owls.

The flight patterns of birds can be very distinctive and will give you important clues to what they are.

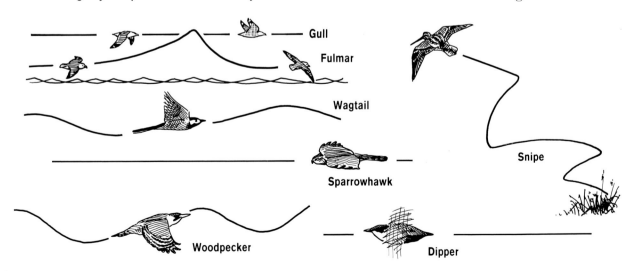

Gull
Fulmar
Wagtail
Sparrowhawk
Snipe
Woodpecker
Dipper

At migration times, be prepared for the unusual, especially after strong winds. This Little Auk (above) should have been far out in the North Sea but gales brought it far inland to rest in someone's pond!

Reedbeds and marshes will attract Swallows and harriers. Birds of prey will also be interested in the roost sites of small birds so look out for Sparrowhawks at Starling roosts or Hobbies at Swallow roosts (in the summer).

Some aspects of a bird's behaviour can give it away, even if it is not actually there. A pile of broken snail shells, for example, is a sign that a Song Thrush has been about. Pellets are coughed up by many birds and are left behind under roosting sites. Owls are well-known for doing this, but other birds produce pellets, too, such as gulls and crows. These are more difficult to find, though, because they break up very easily.

You can identify some birds almost entirely from watching how they behave. You don't need to see all the plumage detail of a Skylark when it is performing its distinctive song flight to know what it is. Indeed, it is when Skylarks have stopped singing and have moved to the coast in winter that they are sometimes misidentified as Shore Larks or Woodlarks by over enthusiastic birdwatchers who are not familiar with these birds in winter.

Some birds can be identified by behaviour alone. The Skylark's song flight is unique. You do not need to see the finer details of its plumage to know what it is.

A bird will usually feed in a way that suits its habitat and way of life, but if a bird migrates it may find itself feeding in unusual places. This is not usually a problem for birds but it can be for a birdwatcher! Even a familiar bird can look quite different if you see it in unfamiliar surroundings. Flying out of the top of an elder bush to catch flies is fairly normal behaviour for a Willow Warbler, but if you saw a Reed Warbler doing this and the elder bush was nowhere near a reedbed, you would probably be a bit surprised. During migration birds can turn up anywhere so do be wary and don't jump to conclusions. Watch how they behave!

CALLS AND SONG

Taking the time to learn bird songs and calls is very useful. Not everyone has a great musical memory, learning a few basic songs will mean you can find a lot more birds than if you ignore the sounds around you.

Learning bird song often seems an impossible task but it will be worth it. Not only will it make spring a more exciting time as you wait to hear your first Blackcap or Willow Warbler, it will help you to locate birds before you could ever hope to see them. Even if you cannot remember the names of all the songs and calls, they can still lead you to birds that you would not have otherwise seen. The best way to learn the different bird songs is to find the bird that is singing!

There are many tapes, records and CDs of bird songs available but, while they are no substitute for finding a bird yourself, they can be useful. Buy with care: if you want to learn the songs of common birds that you may come across in your local woodland, a collection of the songs of the birds of Britain and Europe may confuse you. It will contain the songs and calls of many birds that you may never hear. (CDs are better – you can choose the songs you want to hear.)

To start with, look out for the sound guides that introduce you to the common species and get to know these first. The commentary should tell you what the bird is and there should be text that tells you whether the sound is a call or song. Do not try and learn them all at once, listen to them before and after you go out birdwatching. No matter how good a recording is, listening to birds outside is quite different from hearing them through your stereo system.

Once you know a few of the common birds' songs and calls, you will soon find that any new songs you hear really stand out. If you manage to see the bird responsible, you will find it much easier to remember.

Apart from making you aware that a bird is there, song can mean you can make a positive identification. Willow Warblers and Chiffchaffs can be very difficult to tell apart until they start to sing. There are several other species, too, where hearing a song or call can help, such as Reed and Marsh Warblers and the pipits.

Birds use song to establish a breeding territory and to find a mate but they may also have distinctive calls. Alarm calls are given by most birds when they feel threatened –

A roosting Tawny Owl will get little peace once it has been discovered by small birds. The mass alarm calls (mobbing) will soon tell you where they are.

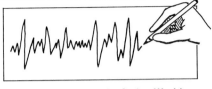

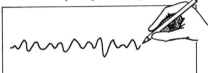

The scratchy song of a Sedge Warbler

The bubbling song of a Reed Warbler.

A DIY SONOGRAM

Sonograms really help you to remember bird songs. Just find a singing bird and draw the sound you hear – as the song goes up and down, so should your pencil. Draw zig-zags if the song is fast and curves if the song is slow.

Some birds sing at night: Nightjars have a strange churring song which you may hear on some southern heathlands. Ornithologists listen for this song to work out how many Nightjars are in an area.

don't ignore them! Often, they will be directed at a predator, such as a bird of prey, and the calls will be your first clue that it is there, so keep your eyes peeled. If you appear to be the reason for the birds' alarm calls, move away from the area because you will probably be near a nest.

Sometimes, you will notice several birds getting very agitated and noisy for no apparent reason. If this is in a wood or group of trees, the chances are that they have found a roosting owl and are mobbing it.

If you are watching birds over an estuary and suddenly a noisy flock takes to the air, look out for a Peregrine or Merlin coming in fast and low, hoping to take a wader by surprise.

Bird songs and calls are unique to the species – they have to be to do the job of setting up and guarding territories and attracting mates. Get to know the songs and you will instantly identify the bird.

Unfortunately, the sheer range of bird songs and calls means that it is far from easy and takes a lot of practice. Any effort you put in, however, will be well rewarded.

Everyone should experience a dawn chorus. Getting up at what seems to be the middle of the night to go and stand in a wood in May seems a bit odd. But, it will be well worth it when you hear the breathtaking sounds of birds competing with each other for territory and volume. This isn't the best way to learn different songs, though, because there will be too much going on. Just enjoy it for the amazing experience it is. (Remember to take an adult with you.)

Willow Warblers (above) and Chiffchaffs (below) are difficult to tell apart until they sing.

TAKING NOTES

Once you know the common birds in your area and your way through a fieldguide, it is a good idea to keep a record of your birdwatching observations. This will help you to remember what you have seen or heard and will make future identifications easier. So much of identifying birds is based on practice and experience that anything you do to build up your own knowledge will be a great help.

A simple notebook and pencil that will fit easily into your pocket are all that you need to make field notes to help you identify unusual birds, record interesting behaviour and help you to remember what you have seen. Some people take extensive notes when they are out birdwatching and then write them up neatly when they get home. This builds up a bird diary and will be a great read in years to come!

Before you reach for your fieldguide, note down any features of plumage and behaviour, the way the bird flies and feeds, as well as apparent colour and fieldmarks. Note any calls the bird makes and whether it was with any other birds. Note anything that might be relevant: time, place and weather are important, especially if you are using your notebook to keep a record of bird numbers and activity in one particular area.

Your field notes need to be quick and simple records. You can fill in any missing names later. Practise doing quick outline sketches that will help you to name the important features. A drawing and a few arrows to key features are a lot quicker than writing everything out. Take particular note of the shape of the beak, tail, legs and wings and how long they are compared with other parts of the body. Note how the bird flies and moves. Does it walk, run or hop? Does it flick its wings or wag its tail? Pay particular attention to any calls because these can be very important.

Good notes should help you to identify any birds you are not sure of and will mean that you can match what you really saw to what is in your fieldguide. You should never rely on your memory alone: without good notes, it is all too easy to forget something that may not seem important or, even worse, to try and make the picture in your fieldguide fit what you think you saw instead of what it really is!

Simple, rough sketches will help you to accurately record what you have seen and remember it. They will also help you to look up the bird you saw in a fieldguide later.

Once you have seen a bird well and made your notes, you can take out your fieldguide and try to match your description to the illustrations. This is where being familiar with your guide will be really handy because you will probably now have some idea which family the bird belongs to.

Start by working out which family the bird belongs to by looking at its general features, especially its beak. It probably will not look exactly the same as the birds in your fieldguide, but that does not necessarily mean that you have found a rare bird! It may be that the bird is moulting or in juvenile plumage. Without taking detailed notes it is easy to end up making a bird fit the description of what you want it to be.

A bird sketch can be 'constructed' from different sized egg shapes to make a head and body. Beak, neck, tail and legs can be added later with the outlines of plumage features and wings.

Not everyone is good at keeping diaries and extensive notes are certainly not essential to enjoying birds. But the discipline of taking notes in the field is a very good habit to get into, especially when you come across a bird that you cannot immediately identify.

As mentioned earlier, instead of grabbing your fieldguide when you see something unusual, record everything you see in your notebook. Try and sketch the bird as well. Mark on the positions of fieldmarks and plumage, etc. Do not be put off if you cannot draw! Making rough sketches really is the best way to make sure you have remembered to note everything. Sketch the beak first and then work your way down the bird. When you have all the details, look in your fieldguide to find something similar.

Again, watch the birds in your garden or park and practise sketching familiar species.

Once back home, you can carry on to finish your sketch as a drawing or painting like this Oystercatcher. Do not worry if yours is not this good!

HABITATS

Different species of birds feed in different ways and will live in the habitat that allows them to feed and breed safely and easily. Knowing which birds to expect to see in any given habitat will help you to find them instead of waiting for one to fly before you first notice it.

The more varied the habitat, the more birds you will see because there will be more food available. For example, a deciduous wood with trees of different ages and areas where old trees have fallen down will have more birds than a conifer plantation.

Before you go birdwatching, find out as much about the site you are about to visit as you can. Read about what to expect and where to look. If you can, visit nature reserves to see some of the best examples of bird habitats. Choose the time of your visit

Inland fields

carefully and you'll have a great day. If you are not sure when best time to visit is or what you can expect to see, write to the nature reserve owners and ask them to send you an information leaflet.

There are some excellent books for bird-watchers that give details of the best places to go to in a particular county. Some even give you a site-by-site guide to the best bird-watching areas in Britain and will tell you the best times of year to visit.

Inland Fields

Land that is not too heavily farmed usually provides a good mixture of habitats for birds and other wildlife. Hedges, trees, fields and woodland provide a wide variety of plants and plenty of food and shelter for animals.

Finches and buntings will feed on seeds and fruits in fields and in hedges. Look out for Kestrels hovering over the fields. They will be looking for voles in the rough grassland at

the edges, where wildflowers still grow. Woodpigeons are common farmland birds, while birds like Yellowhammers are getting rarer. Thick, well-kept hedges provide good feeding and safe nesting sites for many birds, such as Wrens. Look carefully for Red-legged Partridges in open fields. They are very easy to miss.

Coastal Cliffs

The coast can be a great place to watch birds. During the spring and autumn, hundreds of thousands of birds migrate along our coastline and unusual visitors may turn up, so keep your eyes peeled.

In summer, the seabird colonies on northern cliffs are a great place to watch birds. The sheer noise and hubbub is very exciting. Different species nest at different levels: Shags nest among the rocks and caves at the bottom; Razorbills and Guillemots higher up; Kittiwakes and Fulmars higher still and Puffins nest in burrows on the clifftops.

Kittiwakes make a tremendous noise throughout the day, and on some islands, shearwaters take over the noise-making at night. You will often see shearwaters if you watch the sea during the day. Look for long lines of these elegant seabirds cruising above the waves far out to sea.

Another bird to watch out for is the Stonechat. It will often be among the bushes on the top of cliffs. Look at any clifftop hedges and nearby woods for migrants. You may also see pipits and Wheatears in short grass and buntings in hedges and stubble fields.

A coastal scene

Reservoir

Man-made reservoirs and gravel pits can be excellent places to birdwatch, especially during spring or autumn migration. If the water levels are low, you may find waders and Teals feeding near the edges. Out on the open water, look for ducks and grebes.

Some reservoirs have very large numbers of wildfowl (ducks, geese and swans) on them in winter, but unless the site has some well-placed birdwatching hides, you may not get to see them particularly well.

Some of the more recent reservoirs have been specially designed for wildlife and they have varied shorelines with shallow water at the edges and sheltered bays with reeds and trees. Herons will fish from the water's edge or sometimes dive into the open water. Reeds at the edge may be home to Reed Buntings and Reed Warblers and will provide cover for nesting ducks and Great Crested Grebes so keep a good look out. Pochards are common winter visitors but rarely stay here to breed.

If there are any wet fields or meadows nearby, look for breeding waders, such as Snipes and Redshanks, in spring. Otherwise, you will only see waders during migration time, feeding in the mud in large groups.

In winter, there will be more grebes. Keep an eye out for the occasional diver as well. These are usually found where the water is deepest, often by the dam, and they will often stick around if they are not disturbed.

FACTS

It is not just other countries that have special birds. The seabird colonies in north-west Europe are internationally important.

Britain's rocky islands and cliffs are home to hundreds of thousands of seabirds each summer. The largest is the Gannet which has a 2-metre wingspan. Over 160,000 pairs breed here – that is over half the world population!

All seabirds need clean seas and plenty of fish.

A reservoir scene

A river scene

River estuary

Estuaries form where rivers meet the sea and they often provide a good habitat for birds.

Before you go birdwatching on an estuary, it is very important to find out about tide times and keep an eye on the time. Never walk out on to exposed mud. It can be extremely dangerous and you will frighten off any birds that are feeding there.

The muddy shoreline is packed with worms, molluscs and crustaceans – all good wader food. Scan the mud through your binoculars and look for Curlews, Dunlins, Redshanks, Oystercatchers, Black-tailed and Bar-tailed Godwits and Grey Plovers.

As the tide comes in, the waders will start to move up the shore, eventually flying to a safe roost site until the mud is uncovered and they can start feeding again.

Try sitting and watching from the shore as the birds take to the air. You will notice that some species leave the mud earlier than others, depending on how soon their food gets covered up. Oystercatchers and Curlews leave before Dunlins and Knots. At some sites there can be tens of thousands of birds. The RSPB nature reserve at Snettisham on the Wash has roosting flocks of 70,000 waders during winter high tides!

You will often see Cormorants perching on a post or sign. Their habit of stretching their wings out to dry gives them a very distinctive silhouette (and helps their digestion!).

Shelducks are very easy to spot in flight. Their black, white, dark green and chestnut plumage, and red beaks and legs stand out very well against the mud and water.

You may see flocks of finches feeding on the shore or on nearby fields in winter. Look carefully to see what they are. You may be lucky enough to see some Twites among flocks of Linnets.

You will probably also see plenty of Black-headed Gulls or other gulls patrolling the water's edge looking for scraps of food.

So, learn to look at a habitat scene and ask yourself where you would look for birds and what they might be. Then, look carefully and see if you are right.

Scan the landscape with your binoculars, especially along hedges and across fields, and along the water's edge, and the birds will soon start to appear. Your main guide will be a mixture of your own experience and the descriptions and maps in your fieldguide.

If you are planning to go further afield than your local patch to see birds, have a look at one of the many 'Where to Watch' guides to get some ideas. These should be in your local library.

WEATHER

Like all animals, a bird's life is governed by the weather. Learning how birds are affected by it will help you to use it to your advantage.

A bird's behaviour is tied in to the weather all year round and times of drought can be just as serious as very cold weather. During severe winters, birdtables can be a lifeline for many birds and gravel pits and reservoirs with deep water will attract many ducks and grebes because the water rarely freezes.

For birdwatchers, though, the especially interesting time is during spring and autumn migrations. The weather will dictate which birds reach their destinations safely and which ones overshoot and turn up in strange habitats or even the wrong country.

During spring, birds move north through Europe and southerly winds help them on their way. The timing of their arrival is important because if they arrive too early there may not be enough food for them or the weather may be too cold.

Sometimes, early migrants have to turn back from England and wait in France for warmer weather. The birds that breed in the Arctic have to be even more careful because they do not want to arrive in freezing weather. They often stop off on their journeys to feed and wait for just the right conditions.

Migrants fly long distances and try to avoid crossing the sea whenever possible. If they leave one country in good weather, they have no way of knowing what the weather will be on their journey. Winds can suddenly change direction and speed and if conditions are really bad and the birds can no longer find their way, they will be forced to land and wait for things to improve.

In the autumn, many more birds migrate because young birds make the journey as well as the parents. If the weather suddenly changes, spectacular 'falls' of young birds can appear on the coast.

One of the most impressive happened in September 1965, when an extremely lucky birdwatcher was out one morning and saw about 15,000 Redstarts, 8000 Wheatears, 4000 Pied Flycatchers, 3000 Garden Warblers, 1500 Whinchats and 1500 Tree Pipits during one 4-km walk. The total number of birds was estimated at 500,000 on a 40-km stretch of coast!

To see so many birds is very unusual but it shows how important the weather can be. So, pay close attention to the weather forecasts during April and May and from August to October!

Look for an area of high pressure over the top of the North Sea in spring because this should bring winds in from the south. If the weather is clear and fine, many birds may turn up overnight, often well inland. If the high pressure is west of Britain, cold north winds may push birds south or result in a fall on the south coast.

In autumn, strong winds from the west are good news because they may push seabirds close to the west coast and perhaps birds from America. On the east coast, winds from the north-east will bring migrants and seabirds, especially skuas. Again, look for clear weather over Scandinavia and poor weather on the east coast. If this stays, you may find hundreds of birds in woodlands and fields waiting for better conditions.

In autumn, woodlands with Sycamores on the coast are always worth a close look. This tree provides insects for warblers, such as Yellow-browed Warblers from eastern Europe and migrating Goldcrests.

In strong winds, many birds can be blown far inland. It is worth visiting a reservoir where you may see some unusual visitors. After another particularly strong gale, Puffins were turning up inland: one was even found at a bus stop in Bedfordshire!

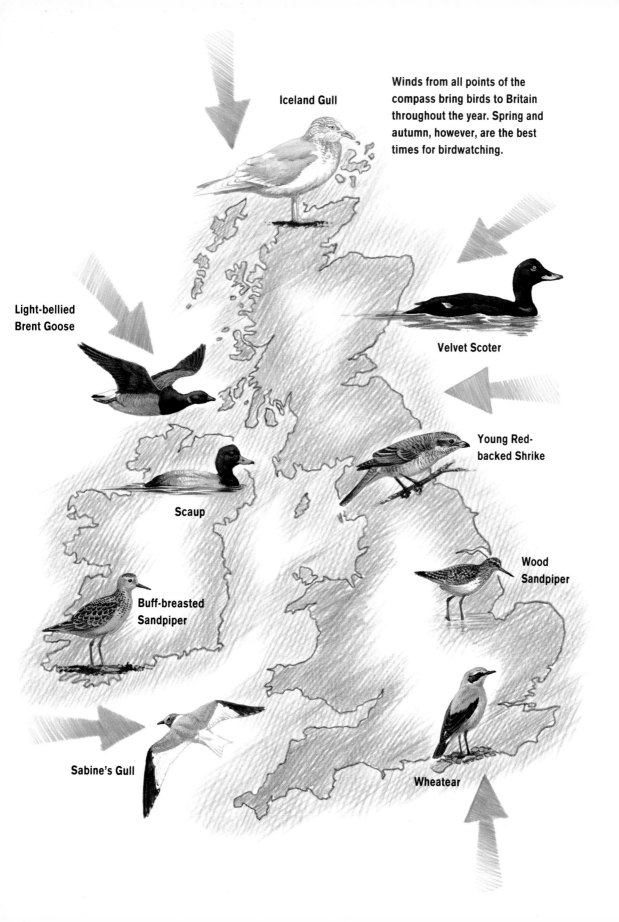

Iceland Gull

Winds from all points of the compass bring birds to Britain throughout the year. Spring and autumn, however, are the best times for birdwatching.

Light-bellied Brent Goose

Velvet Scoter

Young Red-backed Shrike

Scaup

Buff-breasted Sandpiper

Wood Sandpiper

Sabine's Gull

Wheatear

BIRDWATCHERS' CALENDAR

You would not plan a trip to a seabird colony in November or go looking for wild geese in June, would you? For the birdwatcher, autumn begins in July and winter visitors start to arrive in October, while some birds start to nest in February! Knowing what birds to expect to see at different times of the year will help you get the most from your birdwatching.

January and February

This is the coldest time of year and the birdwatching scene is dominated by winter visitors which boost the populations of our resident species, especially thrushes and Starlings. Birds start to feed in flocks and, in some areas, you may see large numbers of finches or larks. Watch for Bramblings in these flocks.

Brambling

Gravel pits and reservoirs are some of the best places to visit. Many ducks and grebes find a safe refuge and good food supply here. There will also be smaller birds feeding nearby or roosting in reedbeds. As well as the regular, large numbers of Tufted Ducks and Pochards, look out for Goldeneyes and Smews.

This is also the time of year when wildfowl (geese, ducks and swans) move down from the Arctic for the winter. If you get the chance, visit a well-known winter wildfowl site, such as the Ouse Washes in Cambridgeshire, Slimbridge in Gloucestershire, Caerlaverock in Scotland or Lough Foyle in Northern Ireland.

The coast in winter is also a great place to visit even though it can be very cold. Birds of prey, such as Hen Harriers, Merlins and Short-eared Owls often move from their moorland breeding grounds to feed on flocks of waders, finches and thrushes that spend the winter on the coast.

Pink-footed Goose (behind) and White-fronted Goose (front).

Some birds, such as Ravens, Herons and Crossbills even start to breed at this time of year.

March and April

Spring is one of the best times for birdwatching with winter visitors leaving and summer visitors arriving, as well as those birds that pass through on their way to the Arctic. Sand Martins, Garganeys, Wheatears, Chiffchaffs and, of course, Cuckoos are some of the first birds you will see and hear, but where they will first appear depends very much on the weather.

Sand Martin (top) and House Martin (bottom)

The south coast is obviously the first place where birds that have migrated from Africa and southern Europe will stop off. If the weather in the south is cloudy or foggy, try to take a trip to areas such as Dungeness or Portland Bill where there may be some early, tired migrants. If it is very clear then you may see migrants far inland, especially on ridges or escarpments along river valleys. Here, Wheatears and Ring Ouzels may make a brief stopover to refuel on their way north.

The first Ospreys will be moving north through the country and may stop off at any small lake to feed, so keep looking up!

Cuckoo

May and June

May sees the arrival of the last of the summer visitors, such as Spotted Flycatchers and Swifts. The breeding season is in full swing and in woodlands the early morning air is full of the sounds of the dawn chorus. On some areas of open heath in the south, Nightjars will be 'churring' as it starts to get dark.

Easterly winds may bring some interesting birds to the south and east coasts and there will be many waders at wetland sites throughout the country. Reservoirs and gravel pits will be good places to see migrant terns and waders, and this is a good time to visit nature reserves, especially those on the coast. May is one of the best months for birdwatching all over the country, but if the winds are from the east or south-east, some unusual birds can turn up, as well as many regular birds.

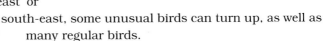

Swifts

Woodchat Shrike

Do not forget to note down the dates of the first summer migrants to arrive at your local patch and watch out for any signs of breeding.

June is not quite as busy as May but it is a great month to visit a seabird colony, such as Bempton Cliffs in Humberside, the Farne Islands in Northumberland or Skomer off the coast of Wales. At this time of year, the adults will be busy feeding their young so there will be a terrific amount of action (and smell!).

At some sites, you can go on special birdwatching boat trips and get really close to the cliffs to watch the birds without disturbing them.

Seeing thousands of auks, gulls and other seabirds is one of the most exciting birdwatching experiences possible.

July and August

This is a quiet time inland because most birds have finished breeding, stopped singing and are replacing feathers before their journey south. Birds can be hard to find, but it is a good time to see butterflies and dragonflies.

Many young birds take to the air, so beware of unusual juvenile plumages. For some waders, autumn starts in July and birds like Green Sandpipers may return to wetland sites. Other waders will start to arrive in August. Some, such as Spotted Redshanks and Curlew Sandpipers may still be in their summer plumage but, as the month goes on, there will be a mixture of summer, winter and juvenile plumages. Take care with identification!

Young Pied Wagtail

Swifts and Cuckoos are some of the first of the summer visitors to leave and August sees the passage of skuas down the coast. Watch out for these 'pirates' as they chase gulls and terns in spectacular dogfights to make them give up their food. You will probably see shearwaters from headlands on the coast and, in some areas, you can go on special boat trips to see them really well.

An Arctic Skua chasing a young Arctic Tern.

Ducks will be in their eclipse plumage at this time of year and can be very secretive and tricky to identify.

Look carefully at hedges and shrubs to see if there are any unusual warblers passing through on migration. Listen out for the calls of birds as they fly overhead. Finches, buntings and pipits have distinctive flight calls.

Remember to leave a good supply of water in the garden for birds to bathe in and drink, especially if it is hot.

September and October

This is one of the best times to see birds, especially if you can get to the coast. Migration is in full swing with many young and adult birds moving south to spend the winter.

Strong north-west winds make for good sea-watching on the west coast and may also bring some birds from America. Easterly winds in Europe may bring birds in from Asia and Scandinavia, as well as large numbers of thrushes, such as Fieldfares and Redwings, and finches and Starlings. All these birds move south to the British Isles for the winter.

The first of the winter wildfowl appear on reservoirs and gravel pits and you may see the passage of larks, pipits, Wheatears and Redstarts at inland migration sites.

Yellow-browed Warbler

Starlings, Swallows and martins will form large roosts at some sites in the evening.

Little Stint

These can be good places to see birds of prey, such as Sparrowhawks and Hobbies.

Strong winds in October will push seabirds far inland, so try and get to lakes or reservoirs early in the morning after a night of storms and you may be lucky enough to see a Kittiwakes or a phalarope.

There are many bird observatories around the coast that offer cheap accommodation at some of the best and most exciting bird-watching areas. You could join an organized trip to stay at one. Contact your nearest observatory for details.

Start to put food out for birds and you will attract more species to your garden. Keep an eye (and ear) open for those flying overhead as well.

November and December

If the weather gets really bad, birds will move to warmer areas and there may be large numbers moving east to west in search of food.

Your birdtable can be a lifesaver and may attract some unusual species, such as woodpeckers, that are having problems finding food in the wild. Provide a variety of food and different types of feeder and you will attract more species.

Redpolls and Siskins will be sheltering in Alder trees by rivers and any large reservoirs will be popular with wildfowl. These birds tend to stay clear of smaller areas of water because they can ice over. Goosanders use inland reservoirs over winter and even the occasional Smew may turn up and stay for a few weeks.

Fieldfare

Pay particular attention to reedbeds at this time of year because they are important winter homes for Bearded Tits and sometimes Bitterns (although these are extremely secretive birds and can be very difficult to see).

If there is a food shortage in Scandinavia, some species will fly south and west and will 'invade' Britain in search of food. Waxwings can turn up in very large numbers and often in towns and on housing estates. In some years, Crossbills flood into the country, but one of the most spectacular 'invaders' is the Nutcracker which normally spends the winter in parts of Scandinavia, Denmark and eastern Europe.

Male Goosander

Smew

THINGS TO DO

The birds that visit gardens tend to be those that would naturally live in woods. A good bird garden will have many of the things that birds would find in woods or hedges: nestboxes replace holes in old trees, and flowers and shrubs provide plenty of seeds, berries and insects for the birds to eat.

Birdtables and feeders can be real life-savers in cold weather and, if you put out a wide range of foods in different places, you will attract lots of different birds.

Some birds feed on the ground, while others prefer hanging off feeders, eating off a birdtable or pecking at fat smeared into bark! Try making your own bird cake: mix bird seed, dried fruit, nuts and kitchen scraps into fat. It is a great way to get rid of old bits of cake or bacon rind.

Make your garden a great place for birds to visit by putting out food, water and providing nestboxes.

A birdtable will attract birds to any garden. The numbers that visit will depend on where you live, but even city gardens can attract several species, such as Starlings, House Sparrows, Blue Tits and Robins.

If your birdtable or feeders are near a window, you will be able to get really close views of birds without disturbing them. As well as watching birds from a window, you could try and get even closer by making your own hide. A simple screen like the one shown in the picture will let you to get incredibly close to feeding birds like Starlings and Sparrows. Seeing them from only about a metre away is a magical feeling. Be prepared to wait a while, though, and keep quiet!

Your local patch

Find a site near where you live that you can visit regularly, easily and safely that has a good mixture of habitats. Rivers, lakes or patches of woodland are good places to try

A simple screen or hide will mean you can get much closer to watch birds without disturbing them.

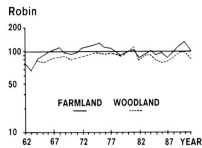

Robin

FARMLAND WOODLAND

62 67 72 77 82 87 YEAR

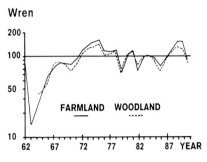

Wren

FARMLAND WOODLAND

62 67 72 77 82 87 YEAR

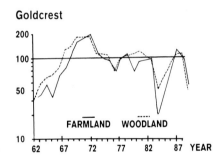

Goldcrest

FARMLAND WOODLAND

62 67 72 77 82 87 YEAR

but any patch of countryside will do. Always remember to tell someone where you are going.

Visit as often as you can and you will soon notice how the birds change with the seasons. Make notes of what you see and record the dates of the first migrants to arrive in spring and leave in autumn, and any breeding birds to compare each year. Watching one site regularly is one of the best ways to learn about birds.

Your local knowledge can be very useful for building up information about birds in your county. A national network of County Recorders collects all the records of birds seen throughout the country. If you are lucky enough to find an unusual bird on your patch, please tell your County Recorder straight away. The address should be in your local library.

Join a club

To get the most out of your birdwatching, you could join a local group of the Young Ornithologists' Club (YOC) or WATCH. You will meet other young birdwatchers, get to go on specially organized trips and find out a lot more about the wildlife in your area.

Taking your interest a bit further can be great fun. It is always rewarding when you see the results of a nationwide survey that you have helped with. One of the easiest of these is the YOC Garden Bird Survey. Thousands of people take part every year and the results are collected by the YOC. They give a picture of how our common garden birds are doing.

You can find out more by contacting the YOC at The Lodge, Sandy, Bedfordshire SG19 2DL. Other useful addresses are on page 47.

The BTO's Common Bird Census gives information about populations of farmland and woodland birds.

GARDEN TIPS:

■ Provide a wide variety of food like kitchen scraps, nuts and seeds at different sites.
■ Plant a selection of plants and shrubs that will provide berries and insects.
■ Provide fresh water.
■ Put up different types of nestboxes at different sites.

GLOSSARY

Albino – A white bird (caused by lack of pigment).

Birds of prey – or 'raptors'. Birds with sharp, hooked beaks and powerful talons (feet).

Camouflage – Colouring, pattern or shape which helps an animal blend in to its surroundings so it cannot be seen by predators.

Coverts – Feathers that cover the bases of flight and tail feathers. The tips of wing coverts often produce distinctive wingbars (such as in Chaffinches). The long 'tail' of the Peacock is really made up of very long tail coverts.

Eclipse – The dull, camouflaged plumage that ducks acquire during moult.

Fieldcraft – The skill and techniques needed to find and get close to birds and wildlife, such as moving quietly.

Fieldguide – A book of bird identification for a particular area.

Fieldmarks – Distinctive, natural marks on birds that help with identification, such as eyestripes, wingbars, forked tails, etc.

Field of view – The area you see when you look through a pair of binoculars, a camera or telescope. In binoculars, the field of view is usually wider the lower the magnification.

Flush – Deliberately disturbing a bird to try and see it better.

Habitat – Where a creature lives.

Hide – Normally a small, wooden, shed-like building positioned to help people see birds closely without disturbing them.

Jizz – A bird's character. A combination of size, shape, behaviour, posture, etc.

Juvenile – A young bird which has its first real feathers after it has passed the fledgling stage.

Moult – The process of getting rid of and replacing worn feathers. Each species has its own time and way of moulting.

Passage – The movement of birds on migration.

Pellet – The bits of food a bird cannot digest brought up through the mouth.

Pigment – The substance that gives colour to feathers and eggs.

Predator – An animal which kills other animals (its prey) for food.

Preening – The way a bird cleans and repositions its feathers.

Primaries – The outer flight feathers that propel the bird.

Resident – A bird that does not migrate.

Roosting – Sleeping or resting when the bird is not actually asleep.

Scapulars – Feathers that cover the area where the upperwing joins the body.

Secondaries – The group of inner flight feathers that lift the bird.

Species – A group of birds that can breed together and that do not usually breed with others.

Territory – An area which a particular bird occupies and defends against other birds.

Twitching – People pursuing rare birds, often travelling many miles to see one particular species, usually a vagrant blown off course.

Vagrant – A bird that turns up accidentally because it has been blown off course, usually as it is migrating.

RECOMMENDED READING

Take a trip to a library to look through these
books:

Birds of Europe by Lars Jonsson. Published
by Helm.

Shell Guide to the Birds of Britain and Ireland
by J Ferguson-Lees, Ian Willis and
J Sharrock. Published by Michael Joseph.

RSPB Book of British Birds. Published by
Macmillan.

Mitchell Beazley Birdwatcher's Pocket Guide
by Peter Hayman.

Birds by Character by Rob Hume. Published
by Macmillan.

*The Macmillan Field Guide to Bird
Identification* by Alan Harris, Laurel
Tucker and Keith Vinicombe.

*Photographic Guide to the Birds of Britain
and Europe* by Hakan Delin and Lars
Svensson. Published by Hamlyn.

Discovering Birds by Rob Hume. Published
by the RSPB.

The Birdwatcher's Yearbook and Diary.
Published by Buckingham Press.

USEFUL ADDRESSES

The British Trust for Ornithology (BTO)

The Nunnery, Nunnery Place, Thetford,
Norfolk IP24 2PU.

Carries out major surveys to find out
the status of British birds. Once you are
confident at identifying birds, contact the
BTO and put your skills to good use. The
information they receive from birdwatchers
like you is very important for the
conservation of birds in Britain. You may
be able to take part in the Common Bird
Census or specialist studies of individual
species, such as the Nightjar.

The Royal Society for the Protection of Birds

The Lodge, Sandy, Bedfordshire SG19 2DL.

The largest wildlife conservation charity
in Europe. Owns over 120 nature reserves,
carries out research, advises Government,
campaigns for conservation issues and helps
to strengthen the UK's wildlife protection
laws. The RSPB is the UK representative of
BirdLife International: the only worldwide
bird conservation organisation.

The Young Ornithologists' Club (YOC)

Address as above

The junior section of the RSPB and is the
largest club of its kind in the world. If you
are between 0 and 18, you can join! Contact
the RSPB for details of how to join and your
nearest YOC group.

WATCH

The Green, Witham Park, Waterside South,
Lincoln LN5 7JR.

The junior section of the Royal Society for
Nature Conservation (RSNC). The RSNC is
the head organisation for the county wildlife
trusts. Contact your local wildlife trust for
details of WATCH activities in your area.
Their address should be in your local library.

INDEX

**The photographs are copyright and are
reproduced by permission of:**

*p.4 B Oddie; p.7 E A Janes (Nature Photographers
Ltd); p.8 R Bush (Nature Photographers Ltd); p.9,
13, 21 (rt), 25 (top rt), 25 (bottom rt), R Tidman
(Nature Photographers Ltd); p.11 P J Newman
(Nature Photographers Ltd); p.17 (top) Bird Watching
Magazine (EMAP); p.17 from Hamlyn Guide to the
Birds of Britain and Europe; p.19 R Revels (RSPB);
p.20 (lt) W S Paton (RSPB); p.20 (rt) R Williams
(RSPB); p.21 (bottom) P Doherty (RSPB); p.25 (top lt)
P Sterry (Nature Photographers Ltd); p.25 (bottom lt)
29 R Tidman; p.31 (top rt) R J Chandler (Nature
Photographers Ltd); p.31 (bottom rt) H Clark (Nature
Photographers Ltd).*